MUSEUM OF
ADVENTURES

FREE ENTRY

No. 0001

Vincent

MUSEUM OF
ADVENTURES

No. 1001

Whenever you see this symbol, there's a puzzle for you to solve. You can check your answer using the decoder you will find, along with Vincent's letters, in the envelope at the back of the book. Place it on the gray fields and turn it until you can read the text.

Have fun reading the story and good luck with all the puzzles!

The Library of Congress Cataloguing-in-Publication data is available;
British Library Cataloguing-in-Publication Data:
a catalogue record for this book is available
from the British Library; Deutsche Bibliothek
holds a record of this publication in the
Deutsche Nationalbibliografie;
detailed bibliographical data can be found under: http://dnb.ddb.de

Prestel books are available worldwide. Please contact
your nearest bookseller or one of the addresses below
for information concerning your local distributor.

The title of the "Museum of Adventures" series is protected by copyright.

© Prestel Verlag, Munich · Berlin · London · New York 2005

Prestel Verlag
Königinstrasse 9, 80539 Munich
Tel. +49 (89) 38 17 09-0
Fax +49 (89) 38 17 09-35

Prestel Publishing Ltd.
4, Bloomsbury Place, London WC1A 2QA
Tel. +44 (020) 7323-5004
Fax +44 (020) 7636-8004

Prestel Publishing
900 Broadway, Suite 603, New York, NY 10003
Tel. +1 (212) 995-2720; Fax +1 (212) 995-2733

www.prestel.com

Translated from the German by Pat Jacobs
Editorial direction: Victoria Salley,
UK/US editions edited by Fawkes Publishing Limited, Twickenham
Design and layout: agenten und freunde, Munich
Origination: w&co MediaServices, Munich
Printing and Binding: Print Consult, Munich

Printed on acid-free paper

ISBN 3-7913-3432-8

Thomas Brezina

MUSEUM OF ADVENTURES

Thomas Brezina

Who Can Save Vincent's Hidden Treasure?

Illustrated by Laurence Sartin

PRESTEL

A Phantom of Many Colors

Who's that?

Who'd dress like that?

Where did this strange man come from? A moment ago the little square at the back of the old sand-colored building was empty. Now a mysterious figure has suddenly appeared in front of the **black-varnished** door as if he has just popped up out of the ground. He's wearing a tall **purple** top hat with a thin limegreen snake coiled around it. The reptile's threatening eyes peer down at you, and it bares its pointed fangs.

The man is wearing a mask of brightly colored feathers above his long beak-like nose. A **rubyred** tailcoat flashes beneath his midnight **blue** cape as he moves, and long pointed orange shoes stick out from his narrow trouser legs.

Who is he? Is he a **phantom**? A **phantom of many colors**?

The mysterious apparition glances around to make sure he's not being watched; then he takes a wire hook from the pocket of his cape and slides it into the lock. He twists it and the door springs open.

Just a minute! Burglars use wire hooks like that to pick locks!

With **metallic blue** gloves he pushes the door handle down and slips into the building, closing the door silently behind him.

The strange man didn't see you. But he certainly broke into the building! Hold on!

Isn't that the door to Mr. Tonatelli's private museum?

You'll have to walk around to the front of the building to make sure.

Yes, it is the museum!

The building has three floors with large windows, and a tall door. Winged dragons and gargoyles stare down at you from the roof. All the lights are on and the door is wide open. Smartly dressed people are streaming toward it from all directions, climbing the wide steps and going inside the museum.

Outside a large sign reads:

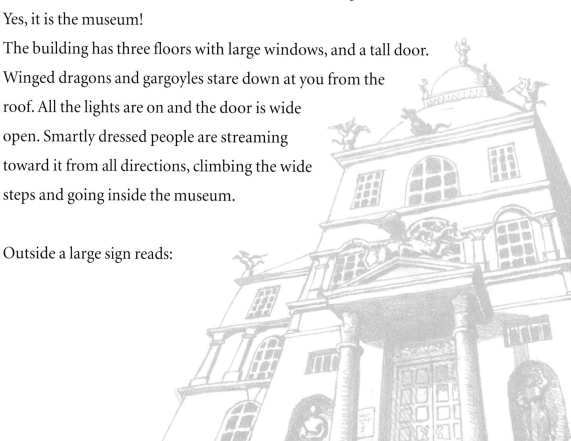

Vincent van Gogh's Masterpieces

Opening today

At one of the top-floor windows you spot the **phantom**. He is standing there, watching the guests through the black eyeholes of his feather mask.

When he catches you looking at him, he quickly hides his face behind the collar of his dark blue cape. Something's wrong here! You must warn Mr. Tonatelli, the well-known owner of the museum.

Starry Night

A young woman with thick-rimmed glasses is standing at the door. Her frozen smile doesn't flicker as she collects the guests' tickets. She looks you up and down disapprovingly. Okay, perhaps you do look a bit scruffy, and she's hardly likely to believe your story about the mysterious intruder.

"This isn't an amusement park! Get lost!" she hisses.

A man appears beside her, his stout figure half filling the doorway. A little brown and white dog dances around his feet. He must have trodden in some paint – one of his front paws is yellow, the other is red, and the back two are green and blue. He scratches at Mr. Tonatelli's trouser leg.

"Stop it, Pablo! I can't play with you now. I have to open the exhibition."

He turns nervously to the young woman and wipes his brow with a red checked handkerchief.

"Have all the guests arrived?" he asks.

She is a lot more pleasant to him than she was to you.

"There are still ten missing, according to my list."

Pablo barks at you and playfully nips your shoelaces.

"So you want to invite a guest too," Mr. Tonatelli says to the dog. He beckons you inside. *"Come on in, otherwise Pablo won't give me a moment's peace."*

The self-important young woman frowns, but Mr. Tonatelli has already grabbed you by the shoulders and dragged you into the museum. There are lots of people chatting excitedly among the wide pillars of the entrance hall. You don't have a chance to tell the museum owner what you have seen because he is already struggling up onto a platform.

"Ladies and gentlemen," he announces, *"the time has come!"*

The crowd falls silent and everyone turns in his direction.

"I would like to welcome you to the opening of this exhibition of Vincent van Gogh's masterpieces."

Pablo whimpers and prods you with his nose. He wants you to follow him through the crowd of well-dressed guests, news reporters, and photographers toward a tall brown door.

Two wide-shouldered men in dark suits are positioned on either side, staring ahead with a grim expressions on their faces. They look like a pop star's bodyguards. The larger of the two is following a fly with his eyes as it gets closer and closer to his face. At lightning speed his colleague snatches the fly and – can it be true??? – puts it in his mouth.

What are these two doing in the museum?

"It is a great honor for me to be able to display some of the world's most valuable paintings in my little museum," you hear Mr. Tonatelli saying behind you.

"When Vincent van Gogh was alive he hardly sold any pictures, and when he did, he didn't even get enough money for them to buy food for a week. Today many of his magnificent paintings are worth as much as a thousand luxury cars."

An astonished murmur runs through the audience.

Mr. Tonatelli points to the brown door.

"Some real treasures are awaiting you in that closely guarded room."

Little Pablo barks loudly and jumps up at the curved brass door handle.

He hangs on to it, pulling it down with his front paws.

The door swings open with a creak, and he slides through the gap.

He starts to **bark** wildly. He's barking at you. He wants you to come in.
The stern guards look at Mr. Tonatelli as if to ask his permission to push
you away. By the time they turn back, you have slipped past them.
Behind the door is a round gallery with a high domed ceiling and no
windows. Brightly colored paintings stand around the room on large easels,
illuminated by spotlights.
Mr. Tonatelli quickly excuses himself and squeezes past the door.
"Pablo, have you gone mad?" he demands crossly.
"We have guests. You can't go around barking like that!"
He wipes the sweat from his brow and his bald head with the **red** checked
handkerchief.
Pablo raises his head and gives a long and plaintive h o o o o o o o o w l like a wolf.
Mr. Tonatelli looks at the painting in front of the dog.
"Are you howling at the moon?" he asks irritably. *"It's only painted!"*
At that moment it happens.
The colors of the painting STARRY NIGHT start to fade.

You're needed.

This can't be happening!

This isn't possible!

Mr. Tonatelli is so shocked he can hardly control himself.

Then a high shrill voice comes from above.

"This is just the beginning!"

There's a small balcony with a stone balustrade up in the dome.

The **phantom** is standing there, pointing at the painting
with his long index finger.

"I can make all the paintings fade away. Every one of them!"
snarls the colorfully dressed stranger, waving his hands in the
air as if to underline his threat.

"But I also have the power to bring the colors back again!"

Mr. Tonatelli gasps for air and stumbles as if he's about to collapse.

"I will make you tremble with fear, as I once trembled with rage!"

The **phantom** pauses and time seems to stand still; then he adds
threateningly, "You'll be hearing from me!"

He pulls up his cape, whirls around, and disappears through a small opening
in the wall.

The two black-suited guards come in. They didn't see the **phantom**
but they spot the blank canvas immediately.

**"What's happened? What have you done?
WHERE'S THE PICTURE GONE?"**

the big guard shouts, his deep voice rumbling like an avalanche.

11

"He's washed all the paint off!" the fly muncher squeaks in a high screechy voice, which sounds odd coming from his wide-shouldered body.

Mr. Tonatelli shakes his head vigorously.

The young woman puts her head around the door.

"The guests are getting restless. They want to see the paintings!" she hisses impatiently, glaring at her boss over the thick rims of her glasses.

The guards plant themselves on either side of Mr. Tonatelli.

"Only you have access to the gallery,"

the deep-voiced guard booms.

"No one else," his colleague squeals.

"You've removed the picture," the first growls.

"Admit it!" they both hiss in unison. The museum owner rubs his hands over his bright red face and leans against the wall for support.

"Where's the painting?" the squeaky-voiced guard demands. His head seems to sprout straight from his shoulders, as if he doesn't have a neck.

Suddenly Mr. Tonatelli gives a feeble smile.

"Oh, how could I have forgotten? I put it somewhere safe."

He gives you a wink. *"We'll go and fetch it right away. Come on!"*

Mr. Tonatelli grabs your hand and pulls you after him. Pablo follows you out of the gallery and Mr. Tonatelli slams the brown door shut. The guests assembled in the entrance hall look at him in anticipation.

"Um... it will be starting soon!" the embarrassed museum owner assures them. He leads you to the end of a long corridor, rummages in the pocket of his gray striped trousers and pulls out a large old-fashioned key, which he uses to open a plain door.

"You have to help me. Please!"

You find yourself in a narrow room lined from floor to ceiling with shelves full of paint pots, brushes, palettes, rolls of paper, pencils, crayons, and jars of luminous powder. There is just enough space for one person to move between them. The smell that greets you is a mixture of fresh paint and ancient books.

Mr. Tonatelli grasps you by the shoulders and stares intently into your eyes.

"Listen, this museum may be small but it holds a great secret. It is the MUSEUM OF ADVENTURES. *I will show you everything later, but first I have an important task for you. It's something I can't undertake myself. Are you ready for a journey into the past?"*

A journey into the past? How can this be possible?

Then again, you're always ready for an adventure.

Without waiting for an answer, Mr. Tonatelli walks over to a pendulum clock between two sets of shelves, takes it from its hook and hangs it on a nearby shelf. The narrow stretch of wall between the shelves opens to the left and right like the doors of an elevator.

"Get into the Elevator of Paintings. It will take you to Vincent van Gogh," Mr. Tonatelli tells you, as if this were a totally normal elevator taking you up to the third floor.

"Ask him to lend you the painting. We need it here urgently."

This is all really confusing!

Pablo is barking at your feet. It sounds as if he's saying,

"Don't worry, I'm coming too."

Mr. Tonatelli pulls open a drawer and takes out a magnifying glass with a brass handle. He turns and hands it to you.

"Take this with you. Then I can send you messages. They will be hidden, but you will know one has arrived when you hear a buzzing sound. Then you can read them through this magnifying glass. If Pablo barks three times, turn the handle of the magnifying glass."

You don't find out what this will do because Mr. Tonatelli is busy reaching for a paper bag, which rustles as he holds it under your nose.

"Chocolate covered hazelnuts – to give you strength."

Pablo begs for a chocolate and his master throws him one, which he catches skillfully. You take one too.

Then Mr. Tonatelli shoves you toward the gap in the wall. It's so narrow you have to squeeze through sideways. *"I'd get stuck, you see,"* Mr. Tonatelli admits with a shrug. The doors close behind you with a hiss.

The elevator takes off.

It's very **cramped** inside the elevator. You are standing in a small hexagonal glass cylinder with matte, dirty gray panes. You can't see any buttons to press. How does the elevator know where to stop? Then you hear a buzz. Pablo whimpers and scratches at the glass. You see something moving in the dirty gray surface – could it be a message from Mr. Tonatelli? It's impossible to read with the naked eye. Maybe you should try the magnifying glass. What's that supposed to mean? What is Mr. Tonatelli trying to tell you? Just a minute! Here on the right next to the door there's a colorful mosaic of tiny stones. It covers the whole of one of the six sides of the elevator, from the floor right up to the glass pyramid above your head. There's a buzz and the next message appears in the gray glass.

What do you make of this mosaic? Can you see what the tiny stones actually
are? Is it really true that a single man painted all these works of art?
Vincent van Gogh must have lived to be at least a hundred years old.
But where is STARRY NIGHT?

Pablo gives you an impatient nudge with his nose. He wants you to press
the tiny stone that looks like the picture that faded away in the gallery.
Use the end of the handle of the magnifying glass – it fits exactly.
The stone glides deep into the wall, where it stays, leaving a hole in
the mosaic.
Through the dirty glass panels you see bright lights racing past from the
bottom to the top of the elevator. You seem to be plummeting deep into the
ground. At the same time you hear a shrill whistling noise that gets higher
and higher until it sounds like someone scraping his nails on a blackboard.
Ouch! It hurts your ears.
Pablo is lying flat on the ground
by your feet with his paws
over his ears.
The elevator jerks to a halt.

16

The noise stops and the doors open to reveal a drab room. It doesn't smell too good, it reminds you of a musty changing room.

Where are you?

Curiously, you stick your head out of the elevator.

There's an oil lamp on a simple white wooden table. The flame is small, so the light is quite dim. A man sits on the other side, his reddened eyes staring right at you. Although he's indoors, he's wearing a fur-trimmed cap and a thick coat.

Grim-faced, he glares at you intently.

Slowly he stands up and backs away nervously until he is right up against the wall next to a small window.

A window with **BARS**!

Is he in prison?

A gentle evening breeze wafts in from outside and the moon shines through the bars.

"Go away!" the man shouts.

Is that Vincent van Gogh?

"Go!"

He looks petrified, like a cornered animal.

A blank canvas stretched over a wooden frame stands on an easel next to the table.

It's the same size as the painting Starry Night, which was displayed in the museum.

Various brushes lie on a chair next to the easel.

"Out! Go!"

Pablo stays close to you, his tail down and his ears pinned back with fear. You hear a key in the door behind you. Someone's coming. Where can you hide?

You're bound to be discovered.

Just paint, paint, paint.

The key turns several times. That door was well and truly locked. This has to be a prison! Someone pushes the door hard from the outside and it springs open.

Pablo barks three times and you quickly turn the brass handle of the magnifying glass, just as Mr. Tonatelli told you to.

There's a whirring and buzzing sound; then, before your eyes, Pablo dissolves into glittering fragments until he is completely invisible. So does the elevator.

And so do you! Amazing!

Now you know what happens when you turn the brass handle of the magnifying glass!

A woman in a simple, dark-colored dress bustles in. On her head is a white starched cap, the kind nurses used to wear.

"What's the matter, Mr. van Gogh?" she asks soothingly.

So you were right. It is him.

The painter looks around the room in bewilderment.

"A ghost. Completely white," he splutters, pointing to the easel.

"My paints. He took them."

The woman takes van Gogh by the arm and leads him to a chair.

Once he is sitting down, she searches the room.

"The tubes really have disappeared. Your brother only sent the new ones yesterday. I brought them to you myself."

Van Gogh clutches his head and rubs his hands over the red stubble on his chin.

"Completely white… it was a ghost. He stole them. And then…"

He points in your direction, his hand trembling. The nurse turns, but she looks right through you to the wall beyond. She really can't see you.

"What's over there?"

"Suddenly the wall opened, and a dog and…"

Van Gogh drops his shoulders in despair. The woman strokes his head kindly.

"Calm yourself. You've been painting all day. Your eyes must be stinging. Try and get some sleep, Mr. van Gogh! Have a little rest!"

Resigned, the painter gets up and shuffles to a simple bed.

"But I wanted to paint the stars and the moon."

Van Gogh waves his hands in the air violently.

Another, younger nurse comes into the little room, carrying an empty chamber pot.

"Can I help you, Sister Anna?"

The nurse pulls a simple gray blanket over the painter.

"No, thank you," she sighs. *"He only ever wants to draw and paint, day and night. That's why he's so ill. And no one even likes his paintings. He's hardly sold any of them."*

Can you believe it? Vincent van Gogh an unsuccessful painter?

And nowadays his paintings are as valuable as a thousand cars!

The two nurses give van Gogh a pitying look before they leave the room,

locking the door securely behind them.

A grinding noise tells you that the elevator doors have opened. Pablo brushes

against your legs as he jumps inside. It looks as though it's time to leave.

You'll be returning to the museum empty-handed.

The elevator takes off like a rocket. It flies through the walls and the roof as if

they were made of water. Through the glass floor you see a hilly landscape, lit

by the moon, and a warm yellow light glowing from the windows of a village.

The phantom strikes again.

"He hasn't painted it yet?"

Mr. Tonatelli is almost screaming. Shocked by his own loud exclamation,

he lays his finger on his lips and hisses, "Shhh!" telling himself to calm down.

You are back in the paint storeroom and he is listening impatiently to what

you have to report.

"I had to bring you back. We don't have much time," he says.

While he tries to work out what your encounter with Vincent might mean,

he paces up and down between the shelves, wiping his brow with the **red**

checked handkerchief.

"The elevator should have taken you to the finished painting, but it

wasn't there, and a ghost is supposed to have stolen the paints..."

Mr. Tonatelli stands still for a moment and knits his eyebrows together so they form a single gray bush.

"I've got it! This phantom ghost has an assistant, who knows how to travel through time. The assistant visited Vincent van Gogh, just as you did, and took away his paints. Van Gogh can't paint **STARRY NIGHT***, so the canvas remains blank. Therefore, the picture cannot exist today either – so it fades and disappears."*

To save the picture van Gogh must get his paints back; otherwise, it will be lost forever.

"We must find this ghost phantom – and his assistant too!"

Mr. Tonatelli explains, sounding just like a detective superintendent.

Pablo sits at your feet, listening attentively, his head on one side.

Was that really a prison where you found van Gogh?

Mr. Tonatelli shakes his head.

"No, it was a mental hospital. An asylum."

Pablo makes a questioning sound, as if he can't believe it.

"Vincent took himself there. He did crazy things sometimes, and some people were even afraid of him."

Mr. Tonatelli takes a hand mirror from a shelf. Its frame contains a number of tiny wheels that can be set to show different letters, but Mr. Tonatelli's fingers are too fat to turn them, so he asks for your help. They must spell **VINCENT VAN GOGH**.

As soon as the last letter is in place, a painting of a face appears in the mirror. It is the man you have just visited. His right ear is heavily bandaged.

"Vincent van Gogh didn't have an earache, and certainly not in his right ear," Mr. Tonatelli begins to explain. *"He painted his face as he saw it in the mirror. That's called a mirror image. After a fierce argument with another painter, he..."*

Mr Tonatelli breaks off mid sentence to show you what else the mirror can do. As you turn the handle, more self-portraits of Vincent appear.

"Vincent painted himself about thirty-five times – probably because he couldn't usually afford to pay anyone to model for him. He bought himself a mirror so he could study his face properly."

Do you notice something about all van Gogh's self-portraits?

What do you notice?

22

The young woman who was collecting the tickets calls from the corridor.
She sounds agitated.

"Mr. Tonatelli? Are you coming? What are you doing?"

Mr. Tonatelli puts his head round the door.

"I'm just coming. Keep the guests happy. Give them a drink and some cake."

The woman glares over his shoulder at you, narrowing her eyes behind the thick-rimmed glasses. She seems annoyed that you are taking up so much of his time.

"The guests are beginning to wonder why you haven't opened the exhibition yet," she complains and reaches for the door to open it fully.

"I'm coming, I'm coming, Jemima," the museum owner says reassuringly, and hurries past her.

Jemima slams the door in your face!!!

You open it again and follow Mr. Tonatelli.

Pablo bounds along after you.

The people waiting in the entrance hall are chattering excitedly.

Various rumors are making the rounds.

"The paintings have been slashed with a knife!" a serious-looking man reports.

"No, there are rats in the gallery. They have eaten one of the pictures," a woman claims.

The crowd bombards Mr. Tonatelli with questions, but he waves them away.

The bigger of the two black-suited guards has stationed himself in front of the door to the domed gallery to stop the guests from entering.

Jemima clears a path through the crowd for Mr. Tonatelli.

"I hope you've got an explanation for this,"

the guard snarls as he opens the door for him.

Mr. Tonatelli makes sure that you and Pablo can follow him into the gallery, but Jemima has to stay outside to calm the crowd.

Inside the gallery the guards stand next to a painting. All that's left of it are a few lines and shadows.

Evil laughter rings out from the dome.

The fly-eating guard runs back and forth, his head thrown back, trying to find out where it's coming from.

"Is this your way of getting this ridiculous museum in all the newspapers?" the other guard hisses fiercely out of the corner of his mouth. **"You're going to regret this."**

The **phantom's** voice seems to circle the dome before it slowly lands on you, like a swarm of hornets. "My revenge," the voice cackles.

Revenge? For what?

Mr. Tonatelli doesn't seem to have heard him. He is worrying about something else.

"All these precious van Gogh paintings have been lent to me by other museums. If I don't return them I'll be thrown into prison."

He looks over at the guards. *"This pair were forced on me by the owners of the paintings,"* he whispers to you. *"They were supposed to guard the paintings – and what are they doing?"*

What can you do now?

"The elevator should have taken you to van Gogh at the exact time he was painting the picture that has almost disappeared," Mr. Tonatelli murmurs. *"Our 'phantom' must have struck again. Perhaps you can still catch him."*

Off you go. Pablo's right behind you.

You have already left the gallery when the museum owner calls after you,

"It's one of van Gogh's early works. It looks quite different from **STARRY NIGHT.***"*

Well, there wasn't much of it left to see.

You'll just have to hope you can find the right painting.

At least you know how the elevator works now.

Your index finger circles the tiny pictures, trying to find the one to press. To make it easier they pop out and get bigger.

Make a decision!

There's a buzz. Mr. Tonatelli has sent you an important message: You can decode what's written on the picture frames using the magnifying glass, so you know if you've chosen the right painting.

Dear Theo, dear Vincent,

With a sharp hiss you're back in the past.

The hard landing catapults you and Pablo out of the glass elevator.

Pablo is lucky and falls on top of you, but you hit the cold floor.

There's a strong smell of smoke from an open fire, and flames are crackling in the walled hearth.

Where are you? You and Pablo hide behind a low wooden chest and you take a look around.

The room is dark, and in spite of the fire it's cold in here.

An oil lamp dangles from the low ceiling, which has been blackened by soot from the fire.

The walls look quite dirty in its flickering light.

A family sits around a table made of rough wood.

Dirty white bonnets cover the women's heads, and the men are wearing caps.

Their clothes are made of coarse material, which looks hard and scratchy.

They don't smell too good – the sour odor reminds you of a dirty trash can.

The meal on the table consists of just boiled potatoes and tea. The people look sad and seem to be very poor.

You hear the scratching of a crayon on paper. A red-haired young man is sitting in the corner of the room. It's Vincent van Gogh.

His hand is moving so fast it seems to be flying over the paper.

Pablo whimpers miserably.

His paws are colorful for a reason – he loves color and often walks in paint on purpose.

But here in this bleak rustic room there is no color at all. Vincent is drawing with a chalk crayon, but the picture that disappeared was painted!

The elevator has dropped you off too far back in time!

Quick! Get back in and press the picture again with the handle of the magnifying glass. Now you know what it's supposed to be:

The POTATO-EATERS.

Your next journey through time is over in the blink of an eye.

You end up in a small, dreary room. Pablo barks three times and you turn the handle of the magnifying glass.

You and Pablo become invisible immediately. It's strange to feel your arms and legs when you can't see them.

A blank canvas stands on an easel in the corner of the room. Van Gogh is sitting at a table writing a letter. His hand moves quickly as he sketches a ghostly figure without a face.

He writes the year on the letter: 1885.

Theo, my dear brother,
I have something terrible to tell you.
I was disturbed by a ghost who stole my paints – the black and the green that I needed for my picture of the farmers.
I wanted to paint them using the colors of dusty potatoes. I want people to see how farmers live. After all, without them we would have nothing to eat.
I wish you all the best,
Vincent 1885

SEE IF YOU CAN FIND THE LETTER IN THE ENVELOPE AT THE BACK OF THE BOOK.

Pablo is sniffing around at your feet.

He picks up the scent of the unknown thief and runs off, his claws scratching on the wide floorboards.

He whimpers briefly at the door, asking you to open it for him.

Like a trained sniffer dog he follows the scent out into a dark hallway.

Perhaps he can track down the mysterious paint thief.

Someone knocks at the door and Vincent opens it. Unfortunately, you're standing behind the door, so you can't see who it is. Van Gogh says something that sounds like, ***"Thank you,"*** and closes the door. Now he is holding a second letter in his hand. He rips the envelope open impatiently. He can hardly wait to read it.

TAKE THE LETTER OUT OF THE ENVELOPE.

There's a short, insistent **bark** from the hallway – Pablo's come back.

Vincent rubs his hand over his short red hair and tugs at his beard.

He seems very angry. He looks around the little room like a caged animal.

"I've got to get away from here," you hear him say.

He snatches the letter he just wrote and rushes off. As he leaves the room, Pablo runs in. There's no longer any danger of your being seen, so you don't need to remain invisible.

Pablo's ears hang down and he whimpers softly.

He has not been able to track down the paint thief, but he

carrying something in his mouth that he lays at your feet.

metal, a kind of triangular cap, half the size of your finger.

pocket.

Pablo gives a loud bark.

The hunt for the paint thief has been fruitless so far.

What is he planning next?

Unsuccessful yet again, you take the elevator back to

Mr. Tonatelli.

Letters, letters, letters

Mr. Tonatelli and the guests are heading toward you from the corridor. The museum owner has his arm in the air and is calling, *"Come along, ladies and gentlemen. First let me take you into the red gallery, where some very special works by Vincent van Gogh are on show!"*

Mr. Tonatelli gives you an enquiring look. Unfortunately, you don't have any good news for him. Pablo runs into the red gallery after his master, so you follow the group too.

Lots of sheets of paper covered with writing and drawings in black ink are exhibited there in glass frames and shallow display cabinets.

"Vincent van Gogh's dearest and most important friend during his lifetime was his brother Theo, who was four years younger than him," the museum owner announces in a loud voice, so everyone can hear him.

"Theo encouraged Vincent to paint and supported him financially. Here you can see some of Vincent's letters. A lot of them are illustrated with little drawings."

There's an astonished "Ooooh" from the crowd. There are at least a hundred letters displayed in the gallery. How many did Vincent write altogether?

"Guess, ladies and gentlemen! Guess!" Mr. Tonatelli urges the visitors.

If you stacked them all up, how high would the pile be?

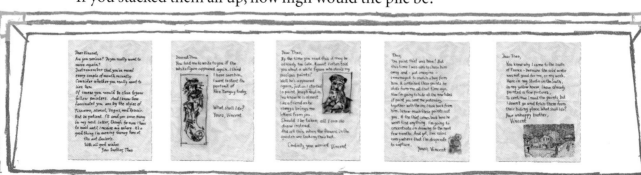

When Mr. Tonatelli gives the answer there's another "Ooooh" from the crowd. Fascinated, the visitors examine the letters. The museum owner pushes his way through the crowd to where you are standing. He listens while you tell him what you have seen and suddenly gets very excited. He looks around the red gallery.

"Perhaps it's possible for Vincent to warn us as soon as the paint thief strikes," he murmurs.

He stops short, staring at the letters. Something has changed!

Can you spot what has happened?

This means that Vincent can send messages to the museum.

Mr. Tonatelli offers you the bag of chocolate-covered hazelnuts but pulls it away again before you get a chance to take one. He throws his head back and empties the bag into his mouth. Pablo barks in protest. Smacking his lips, his master apologizes. *"I need them to calm me down."*

He bends down and whispers in your ear, *"The guards are upstairs, searching everywhere. I hope they find the phantom."*

Someone next to you clears his throat loudly. It's the tall guard.

"Nothing!" he says abruptly. His smaller colleague shoves something in his mouth and crunches it up. It sounds disgusting!

He pulls a brightly colored bag out of his jacket pocket and shows you the candies inside. They look like jelly beans.

"Would you like one?" he asks in his high voice. **"They're fried ants!"**

He sniggers, only stopping when his tall colleague gives him a sharp dig with his elbow. Mr. Tonatelli's red checked handkerchief is soaking wet now, but he carries on using it to mop his forehead.

"Come on," he says quietly, and pulls you out of the gallery, where the visitors are still busy looking at the letters.

The guards watch you suspiciously.

Once you're in the corridor, Mr. Tonatelli makes sure you can't be overheard.

"You must go back and see Vincent. He wasn't always a painter.
Go back to the time when he was painting his first pictures.
Warn him about the paint thief. Tell him that whenever he senses danger he should write to us immediately. We need to know exactly where he is and what he is about to paint. Then we can travel back to the past and finally confront this thief."

It all sounds a bit weird!

"The letters will arrive here in the red gallery,"

Mr. Tonatelli continues.

"Like the letter about the ghost that just appeared."

It's worth a try.

"I'll take you up to the Picture of Time!"

What is going on in this museum?

As you climb the stone stairs, Mr. Tonatelli explains breathlessly,

"When my great-grandfather built this museum he wanted to create unbelievable experiences for his visitors. Don't ask me how he set up all these magic halls and galleries. It's taken me a long time to discover all the museum's secrets myself."

But why doesn't anyone know about these incredible attractions?

"I only let very special people visit the **Museum of Adventures***,"*

the owner explains, and winks at you.

Wow, that's quite a compliment!

Picture of Time

A massive picture frame hangs in a deep, wide alcove. It's at least twice the size of a large door, and it's most unusual in every respect.

The frame ticks. It consists of clocks of every conceivable size, all ticking.

Each one shows a different time, and the hands of some are racing around at high speed.

Inside its frame the picture is just black – not a flat black surface, but a swirling black mist.

"I must get back to the guests and distract them,"

Mr. Tonatelli says hastily, and turns around.

Suddenly he slaps his forehead.

"What a fool I am! You have no idea what this is all about."

He goes up to the frame and beckons you to follow him.

At the bottom are four white enameled dials.

"Set the hands to show the year Vincent van Gogh was born,"

Mr. Tonatelli orders.

Then Jemima calls him again from below and he rushes off.

Mr. Tonatelli calls from the stairs, *"You will be able to watch his life unfold. When he starts to paint or draw, jump into the picture and speak to him! But be careful. He can be a bit of a hothead."*

You hear the museum owner's heavy footsteps stumbling down the stairs. When he's almost at the bottom he shouts a warning:

"You might experience some little storms during your journey through time. You'll be okay, you'll just be carried a few days, weeks, or months further back. It's like hang-gliding."

This is not only a **MUSEUM OF ADVENTURES**, it's also full of amazing surprises. The hands are set. With a deep, resounding ring, the four clocks begin to chime, one after the other. Pablo sits beside you and tilts his head from side to side.

The **black** mist becomes silvery gray, then white, and then it evaporates completely. There seems to be no wall behind this picture. As if through a window you see Vincent as a child, with his family.

A man runs up. *"Vicar! Vicar!"* he cries frantically. *"Come quickly! Old Mara is getting worse."*

Vincent's father nods and says goodbye to his family, leaving them to continue their walk alone.

You and Pablo get caught up in a storm, just as Mr. Tonatelli predicted. Then it passes and you see a shop full of paintings. This must be the time to jump. But Pablo grabs hold of your clothes and holds you back.

Van Gogh, you're supposed to be selling the paintings, not staring at them. SELLING!!! Do you understand?

Goupils & Cie. The Hague Holland

Again you're caught up in a whirlwind. Is Vincent finally starting to paint?

The Reverend William P. Stokes School for Boys Ramsgate, England

Van Gogh, go and collect the school fees!

The people hardly have enough to eat. How can we take the last of their money?

Can you believe it? He's let us off paying the school fees for this month because my father's out of work.

The picture changes again.

And the picture changes again.

Soon the picture changes yet again. It gets darker.

Van Gogh is taking his work as a lay preacher too far. He hardly eats anything and gives away all his belongings. He can't carry on like this.

Vincent still hasn't painted a single brushstroke.
Instead he's tried various other professions, studied theology,
and worked as a lay preacher.

**WHICH THREE PROFESSIONS
DID VINCENT TRY BEFORE
HE BECAME AN ARTIST ?**

A colorful mist swirls inside the frame of ticking clocks; then it parts to the
left and right, like the curtains in a theater, and you get a clear view of a shop.
Numerous paintings are hanging in the large windows. A man and woman
are sauntering past. She is dressed in an ankle-length coat and a tiny hat, and
he is wearing a uniform with gold buttons.

Vincent van Gogh hurries toward the shop with a large portfolio under his arm. He is walking briskly and seems very excited.

"Theo!" he calls, knocking on the shop window. *"I must show you my new drawings."*

New drawings? So van Gogh has already started to draw and paint.

Let's hope you're not too late!

Juuuuuuuump now!

40

Pictures made of dots

You land in a posh shop with a marble floor and square marble pillars. Paintings hang side by side on the white walls, and light streams through the tall windows. Although Pablo doesn't bark, you turn the handle of the magnifying glass just in case. It works, and you are invisible at once. A young man with a well-groomed beard and wavy hair is talking to the couple who were standing in front of the shop window.

"I really recommend this work," he says, pointing to a picture painted in pale colors that depicts an afternoon in the park.

The man in uniform takes a step back, as if the dog in the painting might jump out at him.

"I can't see any brushstrokes," the woman states, bringing her face close to the picture, as if she wants to lick it. "The artist has just painted a lot of dots on the canvas."

"It's the new way of painting," Theo says, trying to encourage her.

Vincent is standing at the back of the shop and beckoning to his brother impatiently. He points to the portfolio with his other hand and mouths to him – he really seems to be in a hurry to show Theo his work.

But Theo gives him a stern look, indicating that he should be patient.

Irritated, Vincent tugs at his shaggy hair.

"I don't like these new paintings," the man in uniform states. "They're ugly. So realistic."

"That's how artists like to paint nowadays – realistically. They want to show how trees, animals, and people affect them. What sort of impression they make." Theo takes a couple of steps to one side and presents another

painting. The couple are not convinced.

"I prefer something more traditional," the man says.

They leave the art dealer's without saying goodbye.

"At last!" Vincent rushes over to his brother and tears open the portfolio. He pulls out a small canvas showing a Parisian street scene.

"It's the restaurant in Montmartre, the Moulin de la Galette," Vincent explains, looking at his brother expectantly.

"It's good. You've really captured the light," Theo remarks, full of admiration, "Especially as you've never really had any tuition in drawing and painting." Vincent gets angry. *"Four weeks at the Academy in Antwerp were enough for me! I didn't need what they were trying to teach me! But I must paint. Like Rembrandt,"* he shouts at Theo, as his brother flicks through the other pictures in the portfolio.

"He's your role model, isn't he? You like his dark paintings."

Vincent lets out a deep sigh and relaxes his shoulders.

"Often painting brings with it sadness, disappointment, and worry. But I'll carry on. I have to paint," he says.

43

"But it's more than that – I feel as if the pictures are trying to force their way out of me."

He snatches the portfolio from his brother and heads for the door.

"See you this evening at the Café du Tambourin."

Theo smiles as he watches his brother storm
out into the street.

You must go after him and warn him about
the paint thief.

Now where's Pablo?

There's a cheerful whimper from below,

as if to say,

"Here I am!"

It's time to go outside
and find Vincent.

Write, Vincent, write!

Fresh, pale green leaves are bursting from the trees lining the streets, and the air is mild, so it must be springtime. Vincent hurries down the wide avenue, busy with horse-drawn carriages, and turns into a narrow side street. Here the houses are very close together, blocking out a lot of the light. The road is unpaved and covered in mud. Vincent runs along with his head down, apparently taking no interest in anything around him.

A shaft of light shoots down from the sky, as thick and as round as the pillars in the museum.

It arrives silently but lights up the dark street like floodlights at a football stadium. Pablo yelps. The bright light hurts your eyes, and you have to peer out through your eyelashes and fingers.

An oval hatch opens at the bottom of the pillar and a sort of door slides up. Out steps a slim figure. Judging by his broad shoulders, you assume he's a man. He is wearing a snow white, skintight suit that completely covers his head, with just two narrow slits for his eyes.

It must be him! This is the paint thief!

Vincent van Gogh staggers backward and shields himself with the portfolio. The white thief jumps toward him and tries to grab the folder. He wants to steal Vincent's drawings. If he succeeds, it means they will disappear in the present day. If these drawings are on display in Mr. Tonatelli's museum, this would make things even more difficult for him.

Pablo gives three short **barks** and a fierce growl, which becomes fainter as he runs off. All you can see of him are his footprints in the mud on the pavement. They are heading for the stranger who is trying to steal the portfolio.

A cry of pain comes from beneath the white mask, and the figure bends down and shakes his leg, but Pablo seems to have bitten him really hard and won't let go. The thief yells and curses. From the modern language he is using you can tell it really is the paint thief!

Van Gogh stumbles back against the wall of a house and observes the commotion wide-eyed.

The white material of the thief's suit tears, and a frayed scrap of fabric dances through the air. Pablo must be holding it in his mouth.

The thief seems to hesitate for a moment and is glancing at the portfolio again. But when he hears Pablo's furious barking, he turns around and runs back to the safety of the gleaming pillar that brought him here.

up
back
shoots
sound it
a sucking
Then with

and disappears until it is just a white dot in the sky.

You hear footsteps behind you. Someone is running.

THEO! He waves and looks very worried when he sees Vincent leaning against the wall, breathing heavily. "What's happened?" he asks.

"A white figure. From the sky!" Vincent vaguely hints at what's been taking place. His younger brother clearly doesn't believe him.

"Vincent, you've had nothing but coffee and brandy all day. You must eat. How many times do I have to tell you to look after yourself?"

"A white figure!" Vincent repeats insistently.

"Here!" Theo presses a few coins into his hand.

"Buy yourself some bread right now. Otherwise you're going to make me really angry."

Confused and ashamed, Vincent nods.

"I really must get back to the gallery," Theo excuses himself.

"But I had a hunch something might have happened, so I had to come after you."

The scrap of white fabric is hovering in the air. Pablo holds it out to you.

You take it from him and put it into your pocket.

Some time after Theo has rushed off, Vincent is still standing there, staring at the spot where the white figure appeared.

You've come to say something to him, haven't you? This is your best opportunity: go on, imitate Theo's voice. Call out what Mr. Tonatelli suggested from a distance.

!esuoh txen eht fo renroc eht ot kcab spets wef a ekaT

It's best if you shout, because when people shout it's more difficult to recognize their voices.

"Write, if you sense danger, write down immediately where you are and what you are about to paint. Never forget that, Vincent! Write!"

Van Gogh really seems to believe that he heard his brother calling.

He gives a snort and nods. You hear him call back,

"I'll write! Writing is much better than talking."

He hurries away, his head down, stamping his feet as if he wants to punch holes in the ground.

"Pssst!" There's someone behind you.

Pablo barks happily and bounds off.

Can you believe it? When you turn around, the narrow street and the houses have disappeared. Floating in the air is a rectangular window the same size as the ticking picture frame, and behind it you can see the corridor in the museum. Mr. Tonatelli is standing in front of the Picture of Time and beckons you to jump back.

So juuuuuuuuuuuuump!

WHICH CITY HAVE YOU JUST VISITED?

Revenge!

An excited murmur rises up from the entrance hall to the first floor of the museum where you are standing with Mr. Tonatelli. Pablo has positioned himself at his master's feet and is licking his hand, which hangs dejectedly by his side.

"It could take us a long time yet to stop this phantom ghost and his white assistant," he groans miserably.

Has another picture disappeared?

Mr. Tonatelli laughs sadly.

"No, fortunately not. The drawing of the **MOULIN DE LA GALETTE** *flickered briefly, but I was the only one who noticed."*

The flickering must have happened when the white figure tried to snatch Vincent's portfolio.

An arrogant, diabolical laugh rings out from the far end of the corridor, which leads off to one side. As the lights are out, all you can see is darkness. Pablo crouches and stares in the direction of the laughter. He raises his head and a threatening growl rolls from his throat.

As if he can cut the darkness in two, the **phantom** suddenly emerges from it and steps straight into the beam of the central ceiling light. Pablo's hackles rise.

Mr. Tonatelli straightens up and mops his brow, using his loose shirttail this time instead of his handkerchief.

The **phantom of many colors**? walks slowly and threateningly toward him. The garish colors of his clothes almost blind you.

Two human eyes glisten behind the dark eyeholes of the feather mask.

"What do you want?" Mr. Tonatelli blurts out.

"You are ruined. Your museum will soon be bankrupt, and then you will have to sell it," the **phantom** says, his voice full of scorn and hatred.

"Who are you?" the museum owner hisses through gritted teeth.

Pablo keeps twitching as if he is about to pounce on the **phantom**, but at the last minute his courage fails him.

"You know me well, even though today you don't recognize me. Just wait. Once I own this museum I will show you my face!"

Mr. Tonatelli points at the staircase.

"Get out! Now!"

50

The **phantom** just laughs contemptuously.

"I was about to leave anyway. But let me tell you something before I go: you can't save any of the paintings. They will all fade away, one after the other. How are you going to explain that? You will be despised throughout the world for destroying such great works of art. Then I will come and save them all. Everyone will love me. Just as you once ruined my life, I'm going to ruin yours."

In the meantime, Jemima has arrived at the top of the stairs. When she sees the **phantom** she lets out a piercing scream.

The figure whirls around so fast his cape looks like a disk as it spins around his body. With a wild laugh he disappears into the darkness. Pablo barks loudly after him, but it's pointless. So he whimpers apologetically and scratches at your leg, the way he sometimes does when he wants to be stroked.

You hear voices from the entrance hall.

"What's the matter? What's going on?"

There's a bang and the sound of people screaming. Then silence. An eerie silence! Mr. Tonatelli goes to the top of the staircase and peers down. When he can't make out what's happened he stumbles down the stairs. You and Pablo follow him.

The door to the gallery where van Gogh's paintings are displayed is open. The blank canvas that was once the painting **STARRY NIGHT** stands on an easel right opposite the doorway. Below it is the brass plate bearing the title, STARRY NIGHT.

The guests stare at the blank canvas with wide, uncomprehending eyes. However, it gets much worse.

51

A shadow appears on the wall behind it – a plump man with a large stomach and a round head.

A woman recognizes him. *"Mr. Tonatelli!"*

Although the museum owner is standing at the bottom of the stairs at the other end of the entrance hall, his shadow is visible in the domed gallery. Mr. Tonatelli is not moving, but his shadow is. Someone must be standing behind the door of the domed gallery and creating the shadow.

Long, distorted arms point to each of the paintings, then finally to the blank canvas. A voice that sounds like Mr. Tonatelli's says,

"They belong to me. All the paintings are mine. I'm going to let them disappear forever so no one else can gloat over them anymore."

The gallery door is slammed shut from inside. At that moment the two guards both try to push through the doorway at the same time and the door smashes into their faces. They stagger back, their hands pressed against their noses. The guests' patience is finally exhausted, and they start shouting wildly.

"Tonatelli has gone mad!"

"Help!"

"I always thought there was something suspicious about him!"

"Save the van Goghs!"

"Let's get out before he starts on us!"

"Call the police!"

Panic breaks out.

A man drags his wife away by the hand. *"Let's get out, before something worse happens. This museum is a minefield!"*

"A minefield!" other people cry, like an echo. They all try to escape through the main door at once.

Less than a minute after the incident, the museum is empty.

Mr. Tonatelli's heavy frame seems to have shrunk inside his suit.

The bloody-nosed guards have planted themselves in front of him.

"I'm ruined!" Mr. Tonatelli says quietly.

The sadness in his voice makes Pablo howl in sympathy.

Vincent's call for help!

It is so quiet in the pillared entrance hall you could hear a pin drop.

Mr. Tonatelli is sitting on a stool with a velvet cushion. Pablo has jumped onto his lap and curled up.

The huge guard with the deep voice is standing next to them with his feet apart and is eyeing them as if they might disappear into thin air at any moment. He is speaking excitedly into his ultra-small cell phone, which is barely visible in his shovel-like hand.

His smaller colleague is emptying the remains of the brightly colored bag into his open mouth.

"Grasshoppers, not fried ants," he explains, crunching away. **"Ants get stuck in your teeth. I much prefer grasshoppers."**

He shakes the empty bag between his fingertips, and it really does have a picture of a grasshopper on it.

The big man with the small cell phone seems to have great respect for the person on the other end of the line, as he keeps bowing during their conversation.

"Very good, Madame. We'll be expecting you, Madame."

When he has hung up he strides over to Mr. Tonatelli, his legs wide apart, like a cowboy's.

"Our boss is on her way. She will deal with you, you can be sure of that."

Mr. Tonatelli looks at him blankly. As if he didn't have enough problems already! Jemima, the museum owner's now somewhat frosty assistant, approaches hesitantly, her coat over her arm. She looks uncertainly from Mr. Tonatelli to the two guards and back again.

"I would never have expected anything like this from you," she begins.

She is behaving as if Mr. Tonatelli really had something to do with the disappearance of the paintings. Well, you didn't like her from the moment you set eyes on her.

There's a timid knock at the museum door. The smaller guard opens it and lets in a tall, lanky young man.

"Hello, Harry, it's a good thing you've come to pick me up,"

Jemima greets him. She has to stand on tiptoe even though he's bending right over so she can kiss him. Harry must be her boyfriend. Pablo raises his head and growls threateningly. Jemima gives him a sneaky kick. What was that for? Mr. Tonatelli holds Pablo's muzzle and tells him to be *quiet*.

"I couldn't get here any faster," Harry says apologetically. He seems very shy. "Where are all the people? Wasn't the van Gogh exhibition opening today?"

Jemima pushes him out. *"I'll tell you everything in the car."*

Swaying back and forth, Harry says goodbye, rubbing his hands against the seams of his trousers.

Jemima turns around in the doorway

"And another thing, Mr. Tonatelli – I'm resigning. I don't want any more to do with you." As she goes down the steps, you hear her say to Harry, *"The old man has gone mad. Completely mad. I was really quite scared."*

Hang on a minute – didn't the **phantom** claim that Mr. Tonatelli knew him, even if he didn't recognize him this evening? So who can be hiding behind the mask?

Does Mr. Tonatelli have any enemies?

The museum owner shakes his head slowly.

"Who would want to do such a thing to me? I have no explanation for this!"

Pablo struggles from Mr. Tonatelli's grasp, jumps to the floor, and runs off.

His ears are pricked up attentively. He seems to have heard something.

Mr. Tonatelli's eyes follow him expectantly.

Just a minute!

You've just realized something else about this **phantom of many colors** ? – he seems to know his way around the museum!

The way he appears and disappears proves it.

So it could be someone Mr. Tonatelli really does know – a person who is always going in and out.

"What?" Mr. Tonatelli suddenly gets breathless and pulls his collar open. *"Impossible!"*

Pablo bounds back with a yellowish piece of paper between his teeth. He is holding it very carefully, so as not to damage it, and he passes it to you. He must have found it in the gallery where Vincent's letters are on display.

> ## YOU, TOO, CAN FIND THIS LETTER IN THE ENVELOPE AT THE BACK OF THE BOOK.

A quick glance between you and Mr. Tonatelli is enough. You both know what the letter means. The **phantom** is planning to strike again. You must stop him and, better still, confront the white figure! But which painting is the **"ghost,"** who is really no ghost at all, going to target? You and Pablo run into the domed gallery and look at the remaining paintings. Which one might soon disappear?

Papa paint seller

The painting of Père Tanguy seems to be waiting for you in the glass elevator.
It isn't a tiny button on the wall – it's **enlarged** and floating in mid air.
As soon as you and Pablo step into the elevator it shrinks back to postage
stamp size and disappears into the wall before you've even pressed it.

Bright lights race past all around you. The faster the elevator travels, the more
intense they become. You and Pablo disappear into a streak of lightning. This
time the elevator simply sets you down, without a bump and without the
doors opening.

Pablo sneezes violently. Atchoo, atchoo, atchoo!

His nose almost explodes.

It's not surprising. The smell of paint and turpentine is quite overwhelming.

You are in a small shop, surrounded by tall cabinets and shelves.
There are lots of blank canvases on the floor, and tubes of paint; pots, and jars
lie all over the place. And there are brushes of all shapes and sizes, from the
softest hair to the coarsest bristle.

Colorful prints hang on one wall, depicting people in Japanese costume,
Mount Fuji – the highest mountain in Japan – and blossoming cherry trees.
A man in a hat is sitting on a wooden stool in front of them.
He is smiling and his hands are clasped in his lap, just like the man in
the painting.

Vincent van Gogh is standing at an easel in front of him, painting his portrait. He has his paints and is painting – that's a good sign. It means that the picture hasn't disappeared in the present day.

Is the **phantom** lurking somewhere? Or the man in white?

There's no one in the shop, but perhaps someone is hiding in the back room, which is separated from the shop by a beaded curtain. Then Père Tanguy notices you and looks down at Pablo.

"What do you two want?" he asks, smiling. "Paints and brushes? You have to start practicing early if you want to become a master."

It's best just to nod. You don't want to draw attention to yourself.

Vincent carries on painting as if nothing exists but canvas and paint.

"How did you become interested in this paint?" the paint seller asks van Gogh. *"It was the Japanese woodcuts,"* Vincent says, pointing to the pictures behind Père Tanguy with the handle of his brush.

"They are so vibrant and colorful."

"Did you know that they were once used as wrapping paper in Japan?" There's a sharp intake of breath – van Gogh is horrified.

Père Tanguy laughs "Yes, vases and statues were wrapped in paper printed with such images. That's how we first discovered them."

*I practiced by copying this picture.
I love the clean lines and shapes of the Japanese woodcuts.*

Stepping backward, Vincent turns away from the canvas and runs over to a cabinet. He seizes the brass handle of a battered wooden drawer, pulls it right out, and empties the contents onto the counter. Lots of gray metal tubes with colored labels fall out. Vincent rummages through them until he finds what he is looking for. With the tube in his hand, he returns to his new painting. He squeezes the tube directly onto the canvas and spreads the paint with quick strokes of his brush. Père Tanguy's smiling face and his hands are already clearly recognizable, and Vincent has just squeezed the blue for his jacket from the tube.

"The city makes me ill. I would really like to move to the south,"
Vincent says suddenly,
"but Theo would miss me. He would be all alone without me."
"It might do you both good to get away from each other for a while!" the paint seller says.
"You've been living together for so long, it's difficult for a hothead like you."
Van Gogh is trembling with excitement and keeps running his hands over his face and through his hair.
"Think of all the new colors you have discovered," Père Tanguy continues.
He takes a paint box from a shelf.

"Look at the dark colors you once used. And today they really **glow**!"
He holds a second box containing **yellow**, **orange**,
vermilion red, **electric blue**, and **grass green** next to
the first. "Go and live where you find such colors. You will feel happy
there."

Vincent hesitates and tugs at his hair because he can't decide what to do.
As he opens his mouth, a warm gust of air sweeps through the open door.
Vincent and Père Tanguy evaporate into a colorful mist, while you and Pablo
are swallowed up and whisked away. The storm intensifies around
you and then you see the dull glass walls of the mysterious elevator. Where is
it taking you?

There's a buzz and something flickers in the gray glass. A message from
Mr. Tonatelli.

The color code

The elevator's journey through time comes to an abrupt halt …

… but not in the museum

… and not in any place where Vincent van Gogh might have lived

… and certainly not anywhere you recognize!

**In the middle of nowhere
the glass cabin stops.
Or hangs.
Or hovers. Or…?**

Through the glass floor
beneath your feet
you see a
hazy colored mist.

Above you there's nothing but blackness.
Where are you? How did you get here?
And more importantly,

HOW ARE YOU GOING TO GET BACK?

ONLY THOSE WHO KNOW VINCENT'S COLOR CODE ARE AUTHORIZED TO CONTINUE TRAVELING IN THIS ELEVATOR. CRACK THE CODE! OTHERWISE, YOUR JOURNEY WILL BE TERMINATED.

That sounds dangerous! The floor beneath your feet starts to shake as if it might open up at any minute. But what on earth is the color code? Pablo stands up on his hind legs and points with his nose to the ceiling of the elevator. Circles of color glow above your head, together with mathematical symbols. They look like sums, using colors instead of numbers. You must have to solve them.

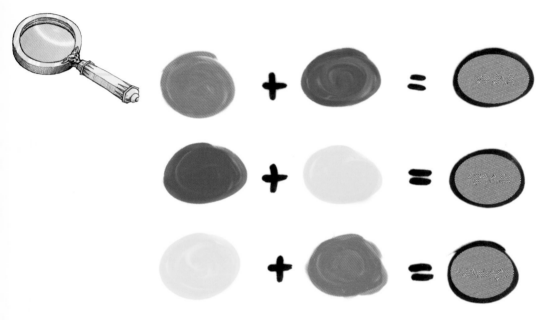

Red, yellow, and **blue** are the primary colors, from which all other colors can be mixed. That much is obvious! But which colors will be produced if they are mixed as shown here?

WHAT ARE THE THREE SOLUTIONS? Hint: You can find Vincent's thoughts on colors among his letters at the back of this book!

As soon as you have solved this puzzle, the colored circles fade and divide into lots of smaller circles.

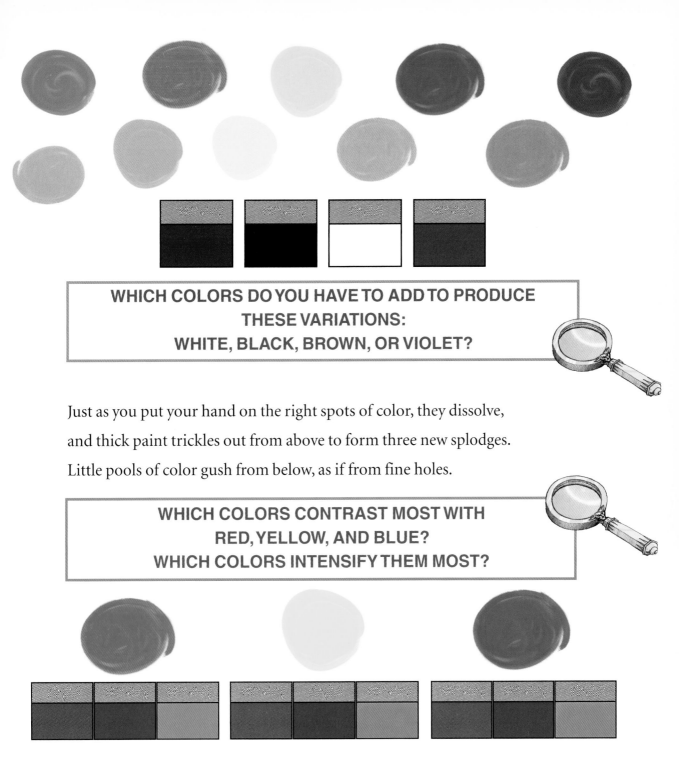

**WHICH COLORS DO YOU HAVE TO ADD TO PRODUCE THESE VARIATIONS:
WHITE, BLACK, BROWN, OR VIOLET?**

Just as you put your hand on the right spots of color, they dissolve,
and thick paint trickles out from above to form three new splodges.
Little pools of color gush from below, as if from fine holes.

**WHICH COLORS CONTRAST MOST WITH
RED, YELLOW, AND BLUE?
WHICH COLORS INTENSIFY THEM MOST?**

When you press the right colors, the elevator hurtles off again. Phew!

One hour, no more!

Back in the museum, Pablo runs straight out of the small room where the glass elevator is hidden. Stretching his nose in the air, he jumps up the steps to the first floor. Sniffing and snuffling, his sensitive nose picks up a scent in the dark corridor from which the **phantom** emerged. You follow him, amazed at how brave he has suddenly become!

Once you step beyond a lamp suspended from the ceiling by a brass chain, there's nothing but darkness, which is very scary.

The **phantom** could be lurking anywhere.

He could jump out and grab you at any moment.

He may have set a trap for you.

Pablo finds his way through the darkness easily and keeps barking as he runs farther down the corridor.

Slowly your eyes get used to the blackness that surrounds you, and you can dimly make out the large old paintings in their heavy, carved frames.

Pablo scratches at one that shows fierce gods on stormy clouds.

He shoves his nose between the frame and the wall and pushes as hard as he can.

The picture begins to tilt. Is it going to fall forward?

No!

It swings open like a door.

Light shines up from below and illuminates the corridor where you are standing.

You are looking into a narrow, bare, gray stairwell.

At the bottom of the stairs is a black-varnished door.

This must be the door where the **phantom** broke in.

So he must have crept up here.

Now Pablo is over on the other side of the corridor, trying to prize another picture away from the wall with his head. It is tall and narrow and shows a veiled woman smiling at you from an open shell.

This painting conceals a secret door too.

Behind it is the stone balcony up in the dome.

Pablo sticks his head between the curved pillars of the balustrade.

You peer over the top to the gallery below. Mr. Tonatelli is trying to explain something to a very small lady with white hair. The guards are standing either side of him, as if to stop him from escaping.

"My dear Alfredo Tonatelli," you hear her say in a tremulous voice,

"I trusted you completely, and that's why I supported your plan to exhibit the von Gogh paintings in your museum. I had to pull of lot of strings to persuade the great museums to lend you these precious, irreplaceable masterpieces."

"I know, I know, Madame Gullerie,"

the museum owner assures her.

"But please believe me, someone is trying to ruin me!"

The guards laugh dryly.

"Don't believe a word he says, Madame!"

"Madame Gullerie, Claudette,"

Mr. Tonatelli pleads,

"it will all be sorted out. Please, give me another chance."

The two guards shake their heads vigorously.

"This is a matter for the police,"

they warn the old lady.

"Dear Alfredo, how long do you need?"

The larger guard doubles up as if he has a bad stomachache.

"Three hours?" Mr. Tonatelli suggests hesitantly.

"I can let you have one hour, no more!"

Madame Gullerie replies.

"Thank you!" The museum owner immediately hurries off.

The guards want to follow him, but the old lady stops them.

"Leave him. We've known each other since school. You can trust Alfredo."

As Mr. Tonatelli leaves the gallery, she gives a little sigh.

"Please don't disappoint me, my dear."

So a very old friendship is also at stake.

The paint thief must be found so that Vincent gets his paints back and is able to paint the pictures.

A NEW LETTER ARRIVED! But how long ago?

Pablo sniffs like mad in front of the pillars of the balustrade, then sneezes violently several times.

Mr. Tonatelli's gruff voice echoes through the museum from the hall below.

He's calling you and Pablo.

The little dog's paint-covered paws trot off immediately.

"Where have you been hiding all this time?" he snaps.

When you tell him about the color code in the glass elevator he just growls impatiently. Then he hands you a piece of paper.

The new letter!

> ## YOU WILL FIND IT IN THE ENVELOPE AT THE BACK OF THE BOOK.

WHICH PAINTING CAN IT MEAN?

It must be of a person. A man or a woman? There are three portraits of people painted by Vincent van Gogh hanging in the exhibition.

A horrified cry from the domed gallery can only mean one thing. The three of you rush to the door and watch as the disaster happens. One of the paintings seems to be exploding. The man's beard and cap jump out and disappear into thin air. His face becomes blurred and his uniform fades.

Too late!

The paint thief will be miles away by the time you get there.

Madame Gullerie has her small wrinkled hands over her mouth and keeps stammering, *"Oh non, non, non, non, non!"*

A mysterious visitor

Mr. Tonatelli is wheezing. He clasps his chest and his face turns **bright scarlet** – it looks like a balloon about to burst. He leans heavily on your shoulder and lets you lead him to a carved armchair in the hall.

He sinks into it with a groan.

"The paint thief... will strike in Arles next."

Mr. Tonatelli gasps weakly, finding it hard to breathe.

Where is Arles?

"It's a place in France – in the south of France," Mr. Tonatelli continues. *"Vincent lived there for a few years. He painted his famous sunflowers there, and fields and bridges, and he lived in a yellow house. The paint thief will certainly turn up there."* His hand trembles as he points to the remaining paintings. *"Hurry, please. Find the paints. Vincent needs them back."*

Barking, Pablo rushes past you toward the glass elevator.

Madame Gullerie and the guards are talking anxiously in the domed gallery. The old lady cries out, as if she is in great pain. A glance through the door explains everything.

> The canvases are almost all white. The colors have disappeared. The most valuable paintings in the world, which have given people so much pleasure, have been destroyed.

This is the worst day of Mr. Tonatelli's life. It should have been his greatest and most wonderful.

The horrified silence that has filled the museum is broken by a knock at the door. The smaller of the guards, who appears to have no neck, strides past you and opens it.

Outside stands a man about the same age as Mr. Tonatelli. His eyes glance inquisitively from left to right.

"Is the owner of the museum here?"

the man asks, breathing heavily.

The guard points to the armchair, where Mr. Tonatelli is slumped.

"My good man, is something wrong?"

the visitor hurries over to Mr. Tonatelli, who looks at him blankly.

"Can I help you?"

"Who are you?" Mr. Tonatelli asks abruptly.

The man, whose face is pink and shiny like a baby's, gives a faint smile.

"You won't remember. We met a long time ago. I came to see you here, in your museum."

Mr. Tonatelli shakes his head slowly. He really can't remember.

The stranger glances around, looking at the walls, the doors, the staircase, and the corridors that lead off the hall.

"It was pure chance that brought me here,"

he declares with a smile that has nothing friendly about it.

69

"But I can see that you're busy, so goodbye. I hope you feel better soon."

He waves his hand in the air like a king acknowledging his subjects. As he turns away from Mr. Tonatelli, the corners of his mouth turn upward in a malicious, evil grin.

Pablo appears from the corridor leading to the paint storeroom – he's come to see what's keeping you. His black nose points in the man's direction. Baring his teeth, Pablo snarls at him. He raises his hackles and crouches, ready to attack, then waggles his hindquarters, unsure what to do next. Then he sneezes, again and again. Atchoo!

Immediately the man starts walking more quickly, until he's at the door. He's suddenly in a great hurry. Pablo storms after him. You follow them both out of the museum.

Night has fallen. The man rushes down the wide steps and along the street, with Pablo hot on his heels.

The stars twinkle overhead and the moon is almost full. A bright beam of light streaks down to earth like a flash of lightning from outer space. It gets wider and wider until it turns into a tube and forms a gleaming pillar next to the statue of a man on horseback in the park. The man hurries toward it.

As before, an oval hatch opens up in the pillar and the paint thief steps out. "What is it?" the man demands.

"That van Gogh is crazy. He threw a full glass at me," the figure in the tight white suit tells him breathlessly. Then he snatched back the bag of paints I stole from him. I had to make a run for it."

The man's eyes narrow into thoughtful little slits.

"Oh well, I got what I wanted anyway. His most famous works have disappeared and just the blank canvases are left. Something must have happened."

The man gives up trying to work it out.

"Never mind. The pictures have been destroyed forever, that's the main thing."

He gives the white figure an appreciative pat on the back.

"What shall we do with this?" the white figure asks, holding out a small white instrument in the shape of a hemisphere.

"Keep it!" The man takes the gadget and presses a button.

The pillar immediately shrinks until it is nothing but a pinprick of light.

The lid of the white hemisphere flips open and the light disappears inside, whereupon the lid closes. The man puts it in his pocket.

"I'm hungry. Let's hope she's made us something to eat!"

The two climb into a silver car and drive off.

PABLO IS TREMBLING. HE WOULD HAVE HAD A
GO AT ONE OF THE TWO MEN, BUT HIS COURAGE
FAILED HIM AGAIN.

Mr. Tonatelli is standing at the door to the museum. He looks ashen. His face seems to have gone wrinkly within minutes. Weakly he holds another letter out to you – it's just appeared.

TAKE THE LETTER OUT OF THE ENVELOPE.

Theo,
The point thief was here! But this time I was able to chase him away and – just imagine – I managed to snatch a bag from him. It contained those points he stole from me all that time ago. Now I'm going to hide all the new tubes of paint you sent me yesterday, together with the one I took back from him. I know how much these points cost you. If the thief comes back here he won't find anything. I'm going to concentrate on drawing for the next few months. And yet, I see colors everywhere that I'm desperate to capture.

Yours Vincent

Going south

In his other hand, which was hidden behind his back, Mr. Tonatelli is holding a roll of grayish brown paper. *"It arrived at the same time as the letter. It was quite a shock – it just fell from the ceiling and landed on my head. But this might be the key!"*

The museum owner unrolls the paper. Pieces of furniture, buildings, trees, and hills have been drawn on it with quick, confident strokes. It looks like a treasure map.

"Find Vincent's precious paints," Mr. Tonatelli urges. *"The map will lead you there. I hope you understand what the drawings mean. Vincent must paint, otherwise the pictures will be lost forever."*

But who is the paint thief? Where can you find him?

> **HEY! DIDN'T PABLO FIND SOMETHING THAT THE FIGURE IN WHITE HAD LOST? NOT LONG AGO YOU CAME ACROSS SOMEONE WHO WAS MISSING THE SAME THING. WHO IS IT?**

Mr. Tonatelli clenches his fists when he hears who the paint thief – the **phantom's** accomplice – might be.

Now it's obvious how the **phantom** knew his way around the museum. He had a good source of information.

"I'll deal with them," Mr. Tonatelli growls so fiercely that Pablo flinches with fear and looks up at him, his tail between his legs. *"It's okay,"* his master reassures him, and violently rips open another packet of chocolate-covered hazelnuts. The brown treats fly everywhere and Pablo is immediately off in pursuit of them.

But there's no more time to lose. Mr. Tonatelli accompanies you to the Picture of Time, where Vincent van Gogh's life is unfolding like a video on fast-forward.

"Jump now!" orders Mr. Tonatelli. A yellow house has just appeared.

So juuuuuuuuuuuuuuump!

You and Pablo are gliding through the air, which feels warm as it flows over your bodies.

Pablo probably looks even more bewildered than you. His paws scrabble helplessly as he tries to find a foothold. It's not like falling out of an airplane without a parachute, more like sailing gently through the air.

You spread your arms and it feels as if you're gliding.

Beneath you stretch green hills and meadows full of flowers.

Nestled between them are small villages with tall, pointed church towers.

The sun is shining brightly in the sky, and the colors of the landscape glow in its warm light.

A small piece of paper wafts through the air between you and Pablo.

Is it a new letter from Vincent that Mr. Tonatelli wanted to you to have on your journey? Pablo is good not just at catching chocolate-covered hazelnuts, but also at snapping up flying letters.

As if someone has simply placed you there, you both land softly in the knee-high grass, surrounded by colorful flowers and butterflies. It really is a letter from Vincent about his precious paints.

> **TAKE THE LETTER OUT OF THE ENVELOPE.**

The treasure map, too, falls down from the clear blue sky. Mr. Tonatelli has thrown it into the picture after you, like the letter.

You wonder what the drawings on the map mean. How will they lead you to the hidden paints?

Pablo's ears prick up, and his eyes shine with excitement. Two faces appear out of the grass a few steps away from you – a boy with his front teeth missing and a girl with a wreath of flowers in her brown hair. Giggling, they look you up and down. Pablo runs over to them wagging his tail and lets the girl stroke him. He always manages to make friends right away.

"Why are you wearing those old-fashioned clothes?" the girl laughs.

You'd better not explain that it's the other way around and it's actually her simple pinafore dress that is old-fashioned. As are the boy's short fringed trousers and blue shirt, which can't be fully unbuttoned and has to be pulled on over the head.

"Your names?" the boy demands.

When you have told him, he introduces himself and the girl.

"I'm Pierre, and this is my sister, Nicole."

Do they know Vincent van Gogh?

Nicole rolls her eyes in horror.

"Maman says we should stay away from him. He's mad."

Pierre pulls a face, as if to say: "These girls are such cowards."

"Yes, he's crazy! But it's fun to tease him."

Excellent! That means they can take you to him.

"He's always trying to get lots of painters to come and live here,"

Nicole tells you as you walk across the meadow.

Her brother laughs until his shoulders shake.

"No one wants to come and live with that hothead. He throws things at people. He slung a shoe at me while I was hiding in some bushes watching him."

"He's a nutcase," Nicole declares.

"The way he paints! Our teacher says you shouldn't paint like that."

Pierre imitates Vincent van Gogh's quick brushstrokes.

"Sometimes he just smears half a tube of paint onto the canvas. The paint is so thick it must take forever to dry," Nicole continues.

"Proper artists spread the paint out. That's what our teacher says," Pierre adds precociously.

Well yes, Vincent van Gogh was different.

He used huge amounts of paint because that was how he liked it.

It gave his pictures something unique.

The two children run off toward the village.

Nicole turns to speak to you. *"Mr. van Gogh is stupid."*

That sounds a
bit mean.

"Come on!" She takes you by the hand and pulls you along after her. You are heading for a little yellow-washed house standing in the shelter of a larger building. You all duck down and creep up to the window, then raise your heads slowly. You are looking into a room where several oil paintings of sunflowers are hanging. Nicole points to one and whispers, giggling, *"He calls that Fourteen Sunflowers in a Vase. Isn't that stupid?"* Stupid? Why?

> **WHY DOES NICOLE THINK THAT THE TITLE IS STUPID?**

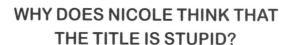

In Vincent's house

WHAT DOES THE INSIDE OF THE HOUSE LOOK LIKE?

Pierre glances up and down the street and runs to the door. It isn't locked and he pulls it open slightly.

"Van Gogh is out," he says, reassuring you.

"We saw him earlier down in the fields. Come on, let's go and have a look around."

Pablo has already put his head round the door, and before you can stop him, he's inside.

What should you do? Go after him!

"*My heart's pounding,*" Nicole admits. "***What if he comes back? He gets so angry!***" she whispers.

Pierre makes a face again, as if to say, "***Honestly, these girls!***"

It doesn't smell too good inside the house – rather like the inside of a trash can. There are other paintings hanging in the room that you saw through the window. Next to a simple wooden table are two chairs with rush seats, a bed, and a small chest of drawers. The floor is a bit sandy and there is dust on the table.

Pierre has already gone into another room.

"***You must come and see this,***" he whispers to you and Nicole. A painting is leaning against the bedpost in the second bedroom. It is an exact reproduction of the room you are looking at, but while in the picture everything is tidy, in reality the room looks quite different.

So this is where Vincent van Gogh washes. There's a soapy smell coming from a bowl containing murky water.

Pierre points to a metal beaker.

"That's what he uses to knock back his coffee."

Nicole tuts, *"You shouldn't say knock back!"*

"You always have to know best," her brother moans, rolling his eyes.

"Van Gogh knocks back coffee, cup after cup. He knocks back brandy too, Maman says."

"Doesn't he eat anything?" Nicole asks sympathetically.

"He just buys paper and paints. He would rather starve. The most important thing for him is to be able to paint!"

Pierre, whose little round belly bulges over the waistband of his trousers, finds it impossible to understand how anyone could go without food.

"And he has awful teeth," Pierre adds, grinning. *"They fell out. The doctor said so."*

Pablo is the first to hear it. He alerts you with a loud whimper.

The front door CLICKS!

Nicole's face turns white.

"He's back. He'll go mad when he finds us."

Even cheeky Pierre is speechless.

Fortunately, Pablo keeps his nerve and runs off, falls flat on his belly, and slides under the bed.

Follow him!

The four of you lie there, peeping out.

It's terribly cramped.

With any luck Mr. van Gogh won't find you.

His footsteps sound heavy. Humming sadly to himself, he stamps around his bedroom. He grabs one of the two chairs and slams it down hard with a furious grunt.

Nicole hides her face in her hands.

Vincent must be angry because he hasn't got anything to paint with at the moment. He grumbles and rants, then grabs a notepad. He's brought something in with him that looks like a reed. Using a knife, he cuts a piece off and sharpens the tip. He dips this reed pen into some ink and scribbles on a sheet of paper. From the noise he makes you assume he is satisfied.

There are dust balls under the bed and the floor is covered with a greasy layer of dust, sand, and something sticky. The dust is getting up your noses.

Pierre is squeezing his closed with two fingers, but even so, he is hardly able to suppress a sneeze.

Vincent van Gogh makes no move to leave the room.

He flicks his shoes from his feet and throws himself onto the bed, which groans under his weight. The mattress bulges down and squashes you.

Then van Gogh jumps up again.

That's better. Now you can breathe again.

The pressure from above has eased. What a relief!

Vincent bends down to look for his shoes.

Oh no, not that.

He's going to look under the bed.

The red beard, the short red hair, and the haggard face appear right in front of you. There's nothing for it, he's going to discover you, and then…

Vincent sniffs hard and rubs his eyes. Then he blinks, but it looks as though he can't see very well. His eyes are bloodshot and full of tears.

He must see everything through a haze.

This is probably why he doesn't notice you. His shoes half on, he shuffles out, armed with paper, ink, and the reed pen. He's going out to draw again.

Painting and drawing are the most important things in the world to him – more important than eating, more important than a family.

Vincent van Gogh wants to paint everything that gives him pleasure.

To show how he feels about people and plants.

It is like an invisible force that continually drives him to paint, paint, paint, paint, paint, paint, and paint.

He needs his paints back!

The fight

After van Gogh has left the house, you lie completely still for a while.

"You never know with him," Pierre whispers. *"He could suddenly come back."*

But Vincent does not come back. Your arms and legs are stiff from lying motionless under the bed. Before he runs off, Pablo stretches his neck, forepaws, hind paws, and back. You all copy him.

There's a buzz. One of the two pictures on the wall suddenly turns gray. Mr. Tonatelli has sent you a message.

Time storm? What does that feel like? You bend down to pick Pablo up and he jumps straight into your arms and licks your face.

A heartbeat later it happens! The floorboards under your feet spring up and catapult you into the air. But your head doesn't hit the ceiling; instead, you glide through it as if it were made of butter.

Even Pierre is lost for words. He stares after you, wide-eyed.

"I want to do that too," Nicole blurts out. All you hear from Pierre is a confused stutter.

Nicole shakes her head wearily and says with a grin, *"Boys, typical."*

The yellow house, the little town and the countryside dissolve into a colored whirlwind. It reminds you of the moment when you rinse your paintbrush in water and the colors mix together.

A sort of tornado has engulfed you and Pablo, twirling you faster and faster and carrying you high over the rooftops. The roaring drones in your ears and ends with a **PLOP**! The storm is over, as if someone has turned off a switch, and you have firm ground under your feet once more.

You are standing in front of Vincent's yellow house again.

But there's a difference. There are no leaves on the trees and a cool wind blows down the street. The sun is lower in the sky, casting much longer shadows. Withered leaves swirl through the air, and Pablo jumps out of your arms to chase them.

"There you are again! Where have you been hiding all this time?"

Waving both arms, Pierre runs toward you. He has a knitted scarf around his neck and a cap pulled down over his forehead.

He gives you a friendly pat on the back.

"Why did you suddenly take off like that? We could have had loads more fun."

Where is Nicole?

Pierre points at the yellow house and pulls a face.

*"She's afraid to come here. You know, there's someone staying
with van Gogh now. Another painter. His name's Gauguin.
But they're always fighting and yelling at one another."*

Together you creep up to the window you peered through before. It's true,
Vincent's not alone. With him is a dark-haired man with a scowl on his face.

"I should never have come!" he fumes.

Vincent stares at him anxiously.

*"We artists must work and live together. Is there a better place
than here?"*

He waves his arm toward the pictures on the walls.

*"I painted the sunflowers so you would feel happy here. And the other
flowers too. I had to paint really quickly because they wilted so fast."*

The man – who must be this
Gauguin whom Pierre and
Nicole told you about – shrugs
his shoulders.

**"Vincent, wake up! Nothing will
come of your dream!"**

But van Gogh sees things
differently.

He lifts up two paintings.

Each shows a chair.

"My chair and your chair!"

"Oh, you and your yellow. I find it sickening."

"It has the strength of the sun!"

Vincent defends his favourite color.

"What have you painted?"

Vincent almost screams.

Gauguin holds up a painting of a man's head.

"I've painted you!"

Van Gogh looks at the picture and his face turns to stone.

"I look crazy there. Mad. And I'm not!"

He is yelling and his whole body is trembling. For a moment it looks as if he is going to hit Gauguin. The other painter steps back, but there's not much space in the small room he occupies in van Gogh's house.

"Those two are always like that," Pierre whispers with pleasure, gloating over the welcome little distraction provided by the painters' argument.

"Forgive me," Vincent says sadly, *"but nobody feels the way I do. Not even you. I am all alone. It makes me feel so angry, so sad, so hopeless."*

His voice has grown louder again. As if he's out of his mind, he runs out of the room and rampages through the house.

"I should never have come," Gauguin murmurs to himself.

"It was a mistake. A big mistake."

The door to his room is slammed hard and crashes loudly against the frame.

Dust falls from the wall, and Gauguin shields himself with his hands. Vincent has returned with a sharp open razor in his hand. Wildly he waves it about in the air.

"You must admire my paintings. You must be my friend."

He runs toward Gauguin, who is standing with his back to the wall.

Gauguin tries to take the razor from Vincent, but van Gogh resists – he curses, yells, rants, and hardly seems to know what he is doing.

"I want you to understand me," he shouts.

Then he gives a cry like a wounded animal.

"You are completely mad. Like your paintings. Your mind is in chaos, just like this house," Gauguin says, grabbing his coat and picking up a small suitcase, which stands half packed behind the bed.

Vincent staggers to one side and stares wide-eyed at his fellow painter.

He gives a soft moan, almost a whimper, and watches motionless as Gauguin charges headlong out of the room.

"I'm going to tell Theo all about this," he shouts on his way out.

Taking big strides, he runs away.

From inside the house comes another roar from van Gogh.

Pierre was crouched under the window and now keeps balancing on the tips of his toes to get a better view. Startled, he topples backward, tries to grab hold of something, clutches your arm, and pulls you over too.

You both land on top of Pablo, who is sitting nearby.

You can see van Gogh's hand through the window. It is still holding the open razor. He pulls it downward. Complete silence follows. Even the birds on the bare branches stop singing. The wind no longer whistles, and not a single voice can be heard in the streets.

Vincent appears briefly at the window. His hand is pressed against his left ear. Blood is running down between his fingers. He groans and staggers away.

"What has he done?" Pierre is frightened now. He keeps swallowing hard, then struggles to his feet and runs off, completely forgetting that you're there. He turns around several times to make sure van Gogh isn't following him. Vincent needs a doctor! His ear must be bandaged.

The front door is pushed open. Van Gogh comes out into the street. He's finding it hard to stay upright. He has a white cloth wrapped around his head, and a red bloodstain is already spreading across it. Holding something in his hand, which is full of blood, he staggers away. The poor man. He must really be desperate, and inside he must be so agitated, shattered, confused and unhappy.

The treasured paints have still not turned up. And as a result many of Vincent van Gogh's masterpieces have disappeared. But what do the drawings on the **treasure map** mean?

Do they show which way you should go?

Where could Vincent have hidden his paints from the thief? Do the symbols on the back of the map mean anything?

Are they letters?

Can you decipher them?

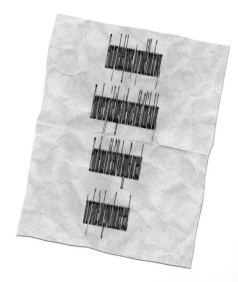

THERE'S A TRICK WHEREBY YOU
CAN READ WHAT'S WRITTEN
THERE! HOW DOES IT WORK?

FIND THE
TREASURE

**HINT: THERE'S A TREASURE MAP AT THE BACK
OF THIS BOOK!**

DECIPHER WHAT IS WRITTEN ON

THE BACK OF THE MAP!

DRAW A LINE BETWEEN EACH PAIR OF OBJECTS,

AS DESCRIBED. THE THREE LINES WILL

FORM A FRAME AROUND THE HIDING PLACE.

"Do you have them? Have you found the precious paints?"
Behind you is the corridor back at the museum. Mr. Tonatelli is teetering up
and down on the tips of his toes, with an old-fashioned pocket watch on a
long chain in his hand. *"The hour is almost up."*

SO, HAVE YOU FOUND THE TREASURE?

YOU CAN FIND OUT IF YOU WERE LOOKING IN THE

RIGHT PLACE ON PAGE 94.

"Only the treasure can save the paintings!"

Of course, you have collected the treasure by now!

You hear an angry voice from the hall below.

"What kind of a daughter are you? A failure, that's what!"

Jemima, her boyfriend, and the man who drove away with the paint thief are standing between the pillars.

Mr. Tonatelli points down at them and shakes his head sadly.

"I trusted her. But she only came to work here so she could spy on me and the Museum of Adventures and help her father to take his revenge on me."

But how come these three are here?

"It wasn't difficult. I had a suspicion that it could only be Jemima. I phoned her and claimed that the van Goghs had all reappeared and, apart from that, there was something that she absolutely had to see. My little ruse lured all three of them here. Fortunately, they brought this with them."

The white hemisphere is lying in Mr. Tonatelli's hand.

"A device that can create a time tunnel. From my grandfather's collection of magical curiosities."

But who is the baby-faced man who dreamt up such a mean, despicable plan, then put it into action?

"His daughter and her boyfriend helped him to deceive me!"

Mr. Tonatelli still can't believe it.

Then he remembers your question.

"The man's name is Harvey Naylor, and he always wanted to be an artist. He showed me his paintings a long time ago, but he never painted what he saw or felt. What he painted wasn't important to him. He just wanted to make money. Because of this, I never exhibited his pictures in my museum."

The man gives a snort of contempt. He can't escape, nor can his daughter or his assistant. The guards are keeping a close eye on all three of them.

"That's why he wanted revenge. He found out about the Museum of Adventures through an old letter from my grandfather that he discovered in a flea market. With the help of his daughter, Mr. Naylor found out all about the museum and was determined to own it. Perhaps so he could destroy more masterpieces – out of envy, because great artists have left us such wonderful paintings, in which we can see and feel how they viewed the world."

The old lady totters out of the domed gallery.
"My dear Mr. Tonatelli, that all sounds completely crazy. The canvases are still blank and your hour is almost up."
The museum owner presses the white hemisphere into your hand.
The time tunnel can take you back to the past, to the precise moment when Vincent van Gogh wanted to start painting and was robbed.
If he gets his paints back, he can create the pictures.
You will return them to him.

You're off!

The first stop is the mental hospital where Vincent admitted himself. It was shortly after he cut off part of his ear. This was where STARRY NIGHT was created.

You give him his paints back, then travel back to the time when Vincent was painting the farmers, then back to old Paris, and finally to the south of France, to Arles.

On the return journey, the time tunnel takes you straight back to the museum. You have just stepped out of the hatch when Harvey Naylor rushes toward you. But it's not you he's after. Instead he jumps into the pillar of light. His daughter runs after him

"No, Dad!" she shouts.

You are holding the white hemisphere with the lid open. With one foot inside the hatch, Mr. Naylor reaches for it, but he is too clumsy and it falls to the ground, landing on one of the buttons. The pillar of light suddenly hurtles upward, taking him with it. Jemima, who had a hold of his arm, is dragged away too. The hissing noise disappears into the distance and the pillar shrinks until it is just a dot of light, which vanishes when it hits the ceiling. The two guards stand there, their heads thrown back and their mouths open. Honestly, their faces look really silly. Pablo looks at them and seems to grin. When he barks they are so startled they both shudder, as if they have seen a ghost.

Mr. Tonatelli lifts up the white hemisphere and turns it between his fingers. *"How can we bring them both back?"* he wonders. *"We've no idea what time they have traveled back to."*

Walking backward, with an embarrassed grin that spreads from
ear to ear, Jemima's boyfriend heads for the door.

At the exit he quickly turns around and runs off.

And so he should!

Madame Gullerie has pulled a tiny pair of glasses with a fine handle out
of her bag and uses them to look around the hall. What is she supposed
to make of everything that's just happened?

You hear Pablo barking excitedly in the domed gallery. There's a surprise
waiting for you there that no one expected.

Several Vincent van Goghs are standing at the easels. One stands in front
of each blank canvas, and they are all painting as if possessed. They are
waving their brushes and are making fast and furious brushstrokes; they
are squeezing paint out of tubes and spreading it on thickly.

The stars and the moon of STARRY NIGHT begin to shine,

Père Tanguy's blue jacket gleams as if it were brand-new, and you can see
what is going through the mind of each person Vincent is painting.

Captivated, Madame Gullerie clutches Mr. Tonatelli's hand.

They both stand there, gazing at the miracle that is taking place.

All the Vincent van Goghs are completely absorbed in what they
are doing. Occasionally one takes a step back from the canvas
and examines his painting. The artist is rarely completely satisfied.

He scolds himself, repaints, and modifies his work.

"He only drew and painted for ten years,"

you hear Madame Gullerie say.

Only ten years?

91

"He didn't start until he was twenty-seven years old," Mr. Tonatelli adds. *"And when he was thirty-seven he decided he didn't want to live any longer and committed suicide."*

ONLY TEN YEARS!

"He produced over two thousand one hundred works during that time," Mr. Tonatelli says, full of awe and admiration.

That means that he often completed a drawing or a painting in a single day.

"He hardly sold anything during his lifetime. Some people said that he painted like a madman."

Madame Gullerie smiles.

"Today we recognize that he was a genius. Nowadays we love the way he handled color, but at the time people found it unusual and disturbing."

"Only his brother Theo believed in him," Alfredo Tonatelli adds.

It is a magical moment in the **Museum of Adventures** to see so many masterpieces created side by side.

Even Pablo, who is sitting next to you, is fascinated.

Mr. Tonatelli wipes his face with a fresh red checked handkerchief.

He has tears of emotion in the corners of his eyes

"Today many of his paintings count among the most valuable in the world. People pay as much for them as for a whole skyscraper!"

"Look, my dear Alfredo, he is satisfied with the paintings,"

Madame Gullerie whispers.

"That we should live to see this, Claudette!"

Mr. Tonatelli tilts his head to one side so his cheek touches the soft, white hair of the little old lady.

Vincent

Van Gogh writes in paint with his brush at the bottom of the paintings.

Not his whole name, just Vincent.

And as each Vincent signs his name, he begins to merge with the canvas.

First his hand sinks into the painting, then his arm, and finally his head and body.

A palette with the remains of the brightly colored paints falls to the floor. Mr. Tonatelli bends down and picks it up.

He lovingly dips his finger into the wet paint.

"A memento for my collection," he says happily.

Madame Gullerie looks at him curiously.

"I keep other things in there that once belonged to great artists. I must show you some time."

"Later," the old lady whispers.

The wonderful paintings are back on the easels.

Exactly as they were a couple of hours ago, when the exhibition was due to open and the **phantom** first appeared.

Wasn't he an incredible man, that Vincent van Gogh?

"But wasn't he very unhappy?" Mr. Tonatelli asks quietly.

The old lady looks at him. *"Look how his paintings glow and make us happy! Look how much joy he has brought us! Perhaps they were his way of smiling."*

They are both standing there, quietly, hand in hand.

It's probably best not to disturb them!

It's late, in any case, and high time you went home.

You creep through the hall on tiptoe and leave the museum.

As you put your hand in your pocket, you feel something hard –

the metal tip of a cowboy boot!

Pablo's claws scratch on the stone floor behind you. He has followed you.

There's something in his mouth, which he holds out to you.

It's a ticket.

Pablo looks at you faithfully. **"You'll come back soon, won't you..."**

he seems to be asking, *"back to the* **MUSEUM OF ADVENTURES!"**

94